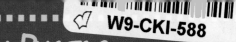

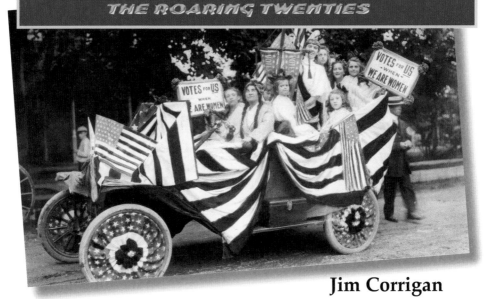

THE 1920s

DECADE IN PHOTOS

THE ROARING TWENTIES

Jim Corrigan

E

Enslow Publishers, Inc.

40 Industrial Road
Box 398
Berkeley Heights, NJ 07922
USA

http://www.enslow.com

Library of Congress Cataloging-in-Publication Data

Corrigan, Jim.
  The 1920s decade in photos : the Roaring Twenties / by Jim Corrigan.
    p. cm. — (Amazing decades in photos)
  Includes bibliographical references and index.
  Summary: "Middle school readers will find out about the important world, national, and cultural developments of the decade 1920-1929"—Provided by publisher.
  ISBN-13: 978-0-7660-3131-9
  ISBN-10: 0-7660-3131-4
  1. United States—History—1919-1933—Pictorial works—Juvenile literature. 2. History, Modern—20th century—Pictorial works—Juvenile literature. 3. Nineteen twenties—Pictorial works—Juvenile literature. I. Title. II. Title: Nineteen twenties decade in photos.
  E785.C67 2009
  973.91'5—dc22

                                                                                        2008042903

Printed in the United States of America.

092009 Lake Book Manufacturing, Inc., Melrose Park, IL

10 9 8 7 6 5 4 3 2 1

To Our Readers: We have done our best to make sure all Internet Addresses in this book were active and appropriate when we went to press. However, the author and the publisher have no control over and assume no liability for the material available on those Internet sites or on other Web sites they may link to. Any comments or suggestions can be sent by email to comments@enslow.com or to the address on the back cover.

Every effort has been made to locate all copyright holders of material used in this book. If any errors or omissions have occurred, corrections will be made in future editions of this book.

♻ Enslow Publishers, Inc., is committed to printing our books on recycled paper. The paper in every book contains 10% to 30% post-consumer waste (PCW). The cover board on the outside of each book contains 100% PCW. Our goal is to do our part to help young people and the environment too!

Produced by OTTN Publishing, Stockton, N.J.

TABLE OF CONTENTS

This magazine illustration captures the spirit of the "Roaring Twenties"—a time when social attitudes were changing in the United States. During the 1920s a clear division emerged between the growing urban population and the rural, more conservative, folk. Young, urban Americans were more likely to drink illegal alcohol, listen to jazz music, and engage in "wild" behaviors.

WELCOME TO THE 1920s

The 1920s were a time of celebration. A tragic episode in human history was finally over. World War I had ended in 1918. Known simply as the Great War, it was a horrible conflict. It lasted for four years and killed 10 million people. Further misery followed. A deadly flu spread around the world in 1918–19. It claimed more than 20 million victims. Afterward, the weary survivors wished to celebrate. The Roaring Twenties began.

Novelist F. Scott Fitzgerald and his wife, Zelda, in a photo taken during their honeymoon. The Fitzgeralds were among the most glamorous figures of the "Jazz Age"—a term that Fitzgerald created to describe the decade. Most of F. Scott Fitzgerald's novels—including his best-known work, *The Great Gatsby* (1925)—and short stories reflect the social division of the 1920s.

Zora Neale Hurston (1891–1960) was one of the leading writers of the Harlem Renaissance. This was a flourishing of African-American literature and the arts that was centered in the Harlem neighborhood of New York during the 1920s.

Americans had the most cause for celebration. The U.S. economy prospered during the war. Factories became very efficient. They made weapons and turned out supplies for the war. Once the fighting ended, those same factories began making peacetime products. They built washing machines, vacuum cleaners, radios, and other household items. People were anxious to buy the many new products. If they did not have enough money, they simply borrowed from banks. Many people borrowed more money than they could afford to repay. Unpaid debt would become a serious problem by the middle of the decade.

There were other problems. In 1920, a new law made it illegal to manufacture, sell, or transport alcoholic beverages. The law was known as Prohibition. Not all people took it seriously. Many Americans continued to drink alcohol secretly. Gangsters smuggled and sold illegal liquor. Dangerous men such as Al Capone in Chicago grew very rich and powerful. Prohibition sought to reduce crime and improve American morals. Instead, it had the opposite effect.

Many other social changes were taking place during the 1920s. Women finally won their long struggle for the right to vote. They were anxious to use their newfound power. Young women, in particular, became bold and independent.

Other social changes were unsettling. The rich became much richer during the decade, but many poor people did not benefit at all from the country's economic growth. Many Americans became fearful of newcomers to the nation's shores. Laws were passed to limit the number of immigrants allowed into the country each year. Only a small number of people from eastern and southern Europe were allowed, and Asians were kept out entirely. The public also lost faith in its leaders. Corrupt politicians took bribes. The government was rocked by scandals. Finally, the 1920s saw the return of a hate group called the Ku Klux Klan.

The Roaring Twenties are also remembered as the Jazz Age. Jazz music had begun to develop a few years earlier in New Orleans. African American musicians pioneered it. They created a compelling new sound. Jazz spread to Chicago and across the country. It inspired new dances such as the Charleston. Jazz music was very popular in illegal nightclubs, where people went to drink alcohol. The birth of broadcast radio in 1920 also spurred jazz's popularity.

The party would not last forever. Trends that began during the 1920s would help shape future tragedies. An attitude of carefree spending joined with other economic problems. Eventually, this would create a financial crisis known as the Great Depression. Meanwhile, a hateful dictator came to power in Italy, another brutal leader tried to seize control of Germany, and a new emperor took the throne in Japan. These three men, who first entered the spotlight during the 1920s, would later help start World War II.

Despite these problems, the 1920s remains one of the most fascinating periods in modern history. The decade known as the Roaring Twenties still captures our imagination today.

Jazz music developed in the early twentieth century, and became nationally popular after the end of the First World War. It was often associated with illegal nightclubs known as "speakeasies." Jazz became a symbol of youth culture and rebellion during the 1920s.

PROHIBITION TAKES EFFECT

Alcohol, or liquor, is a drug. It affects how a person feels and behaves. Too much alcohol can be dangerous. In 1920, the U.S. government decided to outlaw alcohol. The Eighteenth Amendment to the Constitution prohibited the making or selling of "intoxicating liquors."

The move toward Prohibition began as early as the 1830s. Rowdy saloons existed in nearly every American town and city. These unruly bars often played host to gambling and drunken violence. Some states adopted anti-saloon laws. Eventually, Congress proposed a nationwide liquor ban. The states ratified, or approved, it. Alcohol was prohibited in the United States as of January 16, 1920.

Prohibition reflected the division in American society after the First World War. Conservative, old-line Americans supported the legal restrictions on alcohol, while immigrants and young people were more comfortable with alcohol.

A New York police commissioner watches agents pour illegal alcohol into a sewer, circa 1921.

After a 1922 raid, federal agents pose with a homemade "still"—a device used to distill liquor. Each year of the Prohibition period, the number of illicit distilleries discovered by the authorities increased. In 1920, about 96,000 illegal distilleries were shut down; in 1930, more than 282,000 distilleries were busted.

Prohibition came at a time when American society was changing. World War I was finally over. Soldiers returning from the bloody fighting overseas wanted to celebrate. The U.S. economy boomed. Many people moved from quiet towns to bustling cities. They too wished to have some fun. The nation's mood created an increased demand for alcohol just as it became illegal. Soon, gangsters would step in to meet the growing demand.

Andrew Volstead (1860-1947) was an American congressman. He sponsored the Volstead Act, a law that enforced the Eighteenth Amendment.

THOUSANDS ARRESTED DURING PALMER RAIDS

The Russian Revolution occurred in 1917. It introduced a radical style of government called communism. People feared that communism might spread to America. Their fear focused on immigrants. Some felt that newcomers to America might bring dangerous communist ideas with them.

An Italian immigrant named Luigi Galleani helped fuel the panic. Galleani preached the use of violence to overthrow the government.

During the early 1900s, people known as anarchists tried to encourage poor, working-class Americans to overthrow the U.S. government. Anarchists were willing to use violent attacks to gain attention for their cause. This photo shows a car destroyed by an anarchist bomb on Wall Street, the financial center of American life.

The struggle between communists and nationalists in Russia began in 1917 and lasted until 1923. During this time, Russian communists like Leon Trotsky and Vladimir Lenin encouraged workers in other countries to rise up and overthrow their governments.

In 1919, his followers set off bombs in eight U.S. cities, including Washington, D.C. An alarmed U.S. government started rounding up immigrants it deemed suspicious.

U.S. Attorney General A. Mitchell Palmer (1872–1936) was nearly killed when an anarchist bomb exploded near his home in June 1919. In response to anarchist bombings, he authorized the arrest of thousands of immigrants suspected of being anarchists or communists.

Attorney General Alexander Mitchell Palmer oversaw the mass arrests. Thus, they came to be known as the Palmer Raids. Palmer himself had nearly been a victim of the bombing campaign. One of his aides was J. Edgar Hoover. Hoover would later lead the Federal Bureau of Investigation, or FBI.

By early 1920, more than 10,000 immigrants had been arrested through the Palmer Raids. More than 550, including Luigi Galleani, were deported. At the time, a jittery public approved. Today, however, many Americans believe the sweeping Palmer Raids were wrong. Many of the deported immigrants were guilty of no crime.

SACCO AND VANZETTI

Italian-born anarchists Bartolomeo Vanzetti (left) and Nicola Sacco (right) in prison, 1921. The two immigrants were arrested and convicted for a murder committed during a 1920 robbery in Massachusetts. Many people felt that Sacco and Vanzetti did not receive a fair trial. Despite public protests, in 1927 the two men were executed in the electric chair. Five decades later, in 1977, Massachusetts Governor Michael Dukakis declared publicly that Sacco and Vanzetti should not have been convicted, and proclaimed a day in their honor.

WOMEN GO TO THE POLLS

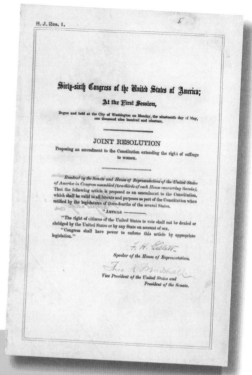

In 1920, women finally attained the right to vote. That right is called suffrage. The Nineteenth Amendment to the Constitution went into effect in 1920. It said that no U.S. citizen could be denied the right to vote because of gender.

The amendment had been proposed and defeated in the past. Women's groups refused to give up. In 1918, they stepped up their efforts to garner public support.

The first page of the Nineteenth Amendment, which gave American women the right to vote. Amendments to the U.S. Constitution take effect when they have been ratified, or approved, by three-quarters of the states. The Nineteenth Amendment was ratified on August 18, 1920, when Tennessee became the thirty-sixth of the forty-eight states to approve the measure.

Alice Paul (1885–1977) founded the National Woman's Party, an organization that fought for women's rights during the early twentieth century.

A group of women and girls display their patriotism while promoting their cause during a suffrage parade, 1920.

One group was called the Silent Sentinels. Its members marched in front of the White House for eighteen months. A suffragist (a person who supported suffrage for women) named Alice Paul was their leader. The Silent Sentinels were insulted by spectators and harassed by police. Several of the women, including Paul, were arrested. Police charged them with obstructing traffic. Instead of paying a fine, they chose jail time.

Public support for women's suffrage was growing. The sacrifices of the Silent Sentinels helped win sympathy for their cause. Congress finally passed the Nineteenth Amendment in 1919. The states ratified it in 1920. That same year, the League of Women Voters was formed. It helped women make informed choices at the polls. The group is still active today.

Italian dictator Benito
Mussolini (1883–1945)
salutes supporters in
Rome, 1925.

MUSSOLINI SEIZES POWER IN ITALY

The 1920s were a turbulent period in Italy. There were few jobs, and many people had no money. The nation was restless. A man named Benito Mussolini saw this as an opportunity. He would use the Italian public's unrest to gain power for himself.

Mussolini addresses supporters during a rally in the historic Colosseum of Rome. In his speeches and writings, Mussolini often promised to restore Italy to the glory of the Roman Empire.

Mussolini came from humble beginnings. He was the son of a working-class couple in rural Italy. As a boy, he showed intelligence but also a quick temper. When he grew up, Mussolini tried to be a schoolteacher. That did not work out, so instead he became a newspaper editor. Mussolini found he had a special talent for swaying people with his words.

With his writings, Mussolini exploited the hopes and fears of the Italian people. He told them that Italy was in danger from communism. He also wrote that Italy could be a great empire, just as ancient Rome had once been.

Mussolini and other uniformed Fascists stand on an outdoor platform in Rome, circa 1922. Over time, Mussolini took over all aspects of Italian government and cracked down on political opponents.

Italy's economic problems and the growing popularity of Fascism forced King Victor Emmanuel III (1869-1947) to appoint Mussolini prime minister of Italy in October 1922. For the next two decades, the king permitted Mussolini to run the country with a free hand.

It simply needed the right leader, he said. Mussolini made it appear as if he had the answers to all of Italy's problems. Many of his statements were exaggerations or outright lies. Regardless, readers savored Mussolini's words. He attracted many followers.

Mussolini organized his followers into gangs called *fasci* (pronounced FA- shee). They wore black shirts and were completely devoted to him. They used violence to frighten his opponents. Mussolini's style of leadership came to be called Fascism. By 1922, tens of thousands of people joined the Fascist movement. They marched on Rome, the capital of Italy. The Fascists wanted Mussolini to be Italy's prime minister. Reluctantly, the Italian king agreed.

Mussolini's power continued to grow. Italy became a police state. Strict laws controlled every facet of a person's life. Newspapers were allowed to write only good things about the government. Anyone who failed to follow Fascist rules received brutal punishment. All that mattered was the glory of Italy and its all-powerful leader. Young people were taught Fascist beliefs in school. Mussolini was in complete control of the country. Nobody dared to challenge him.

The Fascist system became a blueprint for other dictators. In Germany, Adolf Hitler used many of Mussolini's methods to take control of his nation.

FLAPPERS DEFINE FASHION

Before the 1920s, young American women rarely held jobs other than as teachers or nurses. Women were expected to behave demurely and defer to men. However, during the 1920s, young women stepped forward like never before. Known as flappers, these youthful females were bold and independent. Flappers had a unique style and attitude.

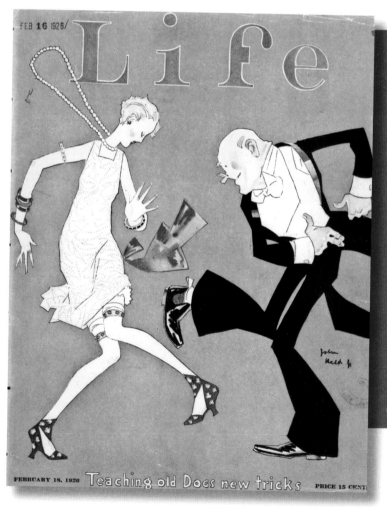

This 1926 *Life* magazine cover shows a well-dressed man dancing the Charleston with a fashionable young woman. The artist who created this drawing, John Held Jr., was one of the most famous illustrators of the 1920s. His illustrations helped introduced the "flapper" image to a wide audience.

Nobody is sure where the term *flapper* came from. It may have referred to a young bird, boldly flapping its wings while learning to fly. It may also have been based on a popular fashion trend. In the 1920s, a young woman often left her overcoat unbuttoned—so that it flapped back and forth—as she walked. It was a statement of her independence. Flappers went to illegal nightclubs called "speakeasies." There they drank alcohol, danced to jazz music, smoked cigarettes, and flirted with men.

The flapper style of dress was unusual. Women tried to achieve a young, straight, almost boyish appearance. They wore dresses that were comfortable, sleeveless, and loose fitting. They kept their short hair tucked beneath a snug, bell-shaped hat called a cloche. This look remained popular throughout the decade.

This flapper, wearing a fur coat and cloche hat, is hiding a flask of illegal liquor in her boot. Flappers were notorious for flouting the social conventions of the time.

THE KKK PEAKS AND DECLINES

Members of the Ku Klux Klan march through Washington, D.C., September 1926.

The Ku Klux Klan (KKK) is a hate group. It was founded in 1866, one year after the Civil War ended. Its purpose was to stop black people in the South from having equal rights with whites. By the end of the 1870s, the KKK had nearly been eliminated. But in the 1920s, it briefly became popular and powerful again.

THE FIERY CROSS OF THE KU KLUX KLAN

D.W.GRIFFITH'S MIGHTY SPECTACLE

THE BIRTH OF A NATION

FOUNDED ON THOMAS DIXON'S 'THE CLANSMAN'

The name Ku Klux Klan comes from the Greek word for "circle." Its members are white Protestant extremists, and they hate anyone whose race or religion differs from their own. Most people reject the Klan's themes of hatred and violence, and for most of its history the group has existed on the fringes of society. However, the 1920s were a restless time in America. People were still shaken by the horrors of World War I. They also feared communism and immigrants. The KKK used these fears to recruit new members.

An early silent movie called Birth of a Nation (1915) portrayed the Ku Klux Klan in a positive light. *Birth of a Nation* was a major hit, and some scholars believe the film's success may have helped the Klan grow during the early 1920s.

The Ku Klux Klan used violent tactics to terrorize and intimidate African Americans. These tactics included ceremonial cross burnings and hangings, or lynchings, of African-American men. During the 1920s, Klan members also attacked Jews, immigrants, Catholics, and communists.

By 1924, the Klan's membership had climbed into the millions. Klansmen held positions of power in some local and state governments. The group also had an impact on national politics. The Ku Klux Klan's revival did not last long. The group's violent nature and corrupt leaders disgusted many new members. They promptly quit the organization. By 1929, the KKK had once again withdrawn into the shadows of society.

PRESIDENT HARDING DIES IN OFFICE

Warren G. Harding was the nation's twenty-ninth president. He had been in office only for about two years when he died suddenly of natural causes. The nation mourned. Unfortunately, his administration would be remembered for scandal and corruption.

The Ohio native was elected president at age fifty-five. He promised to return America to "normalcy," a word that he popularized. Harding felt that the United States should withdraw from world affairs. The idea appealed to voters who regretted America's involvement in World War I. Once in office, Harding

Warren G. Harding (1865–1923) had served in Ohio's legislature and as the state's lieutenant governor before being elected to the U.S. Senate in 1915. In November 1920, he easily defeated Democratic Party candidate James M. Cox, receiving 60 percent of the vote.

President Harding (left) is pictured at a meeting with his top advisors (known as his cabinet).

After President Harding's death on August 2, 1923, his body was returned to Washington, D.C. A public funeral service was held at the Capitol. This photo shows a military honor guard accompanying the president's flag-draped casket.

repealed wartime taxes. He created a federal agency to assist veterans. He also supported tight limits on immigration to the United States.

Warren Harding was an honest man. However, he was a poor judge of character. He gave several friends important government jobs. These people were less honest. They used their authority to make money illegally. When these abuses were discovered, the public became furious. The Harding administration was rocked by scandal.

The corruption embarrassed Warren Harding. It also took a toll on his health. In late July 1923, the president suddenly collapsed in a San Francisco hotel. Warren G. Harding died four days later. Vice President Calvin Coolidge succeeded him.

Vice President Calvin Coolidge (1872–1933) served the remainder of Harding's term, then won a presidential term of his own in 1924.

TEAPOT DOME SCANDAL RIVETS THE NATION

The Harding era had many scandals. Teapot Dome was the most famous. It gradually grew into a national uproar.

The U.S. Navy had set aside oil fields in Wyoming and California. The fields would act as a fuel reserve for navy ships in case of emergency. A huge rock formation that looked like a teapot sat atop the Wyoming field. Accordingly, it was called Teapot Dome. Albert B. Fall was the U.S. Secretary

The Teapot Dome oil field is located on government-owned land in Wyoming.

of the Interior. In 1921 he asked for permission to supervise the oil reserves. President Warren Harding agreed to his friend's request.

Within a year, Secretary Fall was leasing the oil reserves to private companies. This act alone was legal. However, rumors persisted that Fall was accepting bribes for the leases. Albert Fall proclaimed his innocence but resigned his post as Secretary of the Interior in 1923. Congress investigated for years, but could uncover no proof of wrongdoing. The investigators were about to give up. Then they found evidence that Fall had indeed taken bribes. He had illegally accepted roughly $400,000 for the oil leases. The American public was outraged. Albert Fall was sent to prison in 1929. The Teapot Dome scandal was finally over.

As Secretary of the Interior, Albert Fall (1861–1944) was given control over the oil fields at Teapot Dome and at Elk Hills, California. Fall allowed two private companies, Sinclair Oil and Pan American Petroleum, to extract oil from the fields.

This 1924 political cartoon shows Washington officials trying to get out of the way of the Teapot Dome scandal.

:Der Feind ist im Land!
:So wehr' dich der Schand,
:Wie lautet das Feldgeschrei:
:Bayerische Volkspartei!

Propaganda poster, circa 1920, warning about the danger of communism and encouraging Germans to support a Bavarian political party. For Germany, the 1920s were a decade of political instability and economic crisis.

GERMANY SLIPS INTO CRISIS

The nation of Germany struggled during the 1920s. Its citizens were poor and unhappy. Following World War I, Germany became a democracy. However, the country's new government was weak. It could not stop the suffering of its people. Angry young radicals argued for the government to be overthrown. One of the most vocal critics was a man named Adolf Hitler.

Adolf Hitler (1889–1945) is seated on the left of this photo of German soldiers taken during the First World War. Like many other citizens of Germany, Hitler resented the humiliating terms of the Treaty of Versailles. Angry with the new German government, Hitler joined the Nazi Party in 1920.

A respected former general, Paul von Hindenberg (1847–1934), was elected president of Germany in 1925. Hindenberg disliked Hitler, but was unable to prevent the Nazi Party from gaining seats in the Reichstag, or German legislature.

The nation's problems started with the end of World War I. Many Germans were upset over the outcome of the war. No foreign soldier had set foot on German soil. People could not understand how Germany had lost the war. The Treaty of Versailles, which ended the conflict, forced Germany to accept blame for starting World War I. Germany was forced to give up valuable land. This included all of its overseas colonies. Under the terms of the Treaty of Versailles, Germany was required to reduce the size of its army and pay the Allies $33 billion to cover the cost of the war. Its citizens were furious.

The war payments were more than Germany's fragile economy could handle. They created a huge national debt. German money began losing its value. Eventually, it became almost worthless. The German people found it was cheaper to burn cash for heat than to buy firewood. The country fell behind in its war payments. As a result, troops from France and Belgium moved into the Ruhr Valley, Germany's industrial region. By occupying the Ruhr, the French and Belgians hoped to force the German government to pay its war debts.

Many Germans blamed their new democratic government for their problems. They said that their leaders never should have signed the peace treaty. Workers staged protests and strikes. Adolf Hitler fueled their rage. He gave emotional speeches criticizing the government. Hitler was the leader of the National Socialist German Workers Party, which was called the Nazi Party for short. Like Mussolini in Italy, he gained many devoted followers.

In November 1923, Adolf Hitler and his armed supporters tried to overthrow the democratic government. They stormed into a political rally at a beer hall in the city of Munich. They tried to force the political leaders present into joining them. Hitler's "Beer Hall Putsch" failed. He was arrested for treason. However, the defiant act earned him national attention. Hitler used his trial to promote the Nazi Party. He wrote a book called *Mein Kampf* (My Struggle) during his nine-month prison term. The seeds for future Nazi rule were sown.

Upon his release from prison, Hitler continued building support for his Nazi Party. He focused on gaining power through elections. Like Mussolini, Hitler built an army of storm troopers. They were called brownshirts because of the color of their uniform shirts. Hitler used these violent men to intimidate his political opponents. The menace of the Nazi Party continued to grow during the decade. In the 1930s, Hitler would seize total control of Germany.

Hitler attracted followers during the 1920s by promising to build a glorious new Germany. This Nazi propaganda poster carries the slogan "Hitler builds, we help."

SPORTING CELEBRITIES

The 1920s saw the rise of the modern sports hero. Americans came to cherish their favorite players. Top athletes performed before enormous crowds of cheering fans.

The decade is known as the golden age of boxing. Heavyweight champion Jack Dempsey first captured the title in 1919. He held it for seven years. Dempsey was a longtime fan favorite. In addition to great boxing skills, he had a magnetic personality. His thrilling fights drew record crowds and made front-page headlines. More than 120,000 people

Heavyweight boxer Jack Dempsey (1895–1983) was one of the most popular sports stars of the 1920s. Born in Manassa, Colorado, Dempsey was nicknamed the "Manassa Mauler."

watched Dempsey's shocking 1926 title loss to Gene Tunney. Millions more listened by radio.

Also in the 1920s, Babe Ruth revived America's passion for baseball. The national pastime briefly fell from grace during a 1919 scandal. In that year, eight players accepted bribes to lose the World Series. George Herman Ruth brought fans back to the ballpark. They were amazed by his incredible

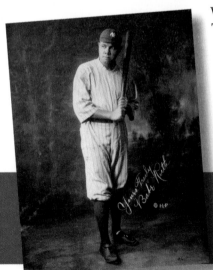

George Herman "Babe" Ruth (1895–1948) was one of the greatest baseball players of all time. This photo was taken in 1920, Ruth's first season with the New York Yankees. That year he hit 54 home runs—more than all but one major league team.

Poster for the 1924 Olympic Games, which were held in Paris. Athletes from forty-four nations participated in the games. American athletes won forty-five gold medals to lead all countries.

slugging skills. Early in his career, the baby-faced Ruth played for the Boston Red Sox. After the 1919 season, Boston's owner sold him to New York. Ruth put on the Yankee pinstripes in 1920. He led New York to seven World Series appearances, including four World Series titles. He also maintained a .342 lifetime batting average and set many records.

The NFL Arrives

The National Football League formed in 1922. At the time, college football was far more popular. In 1925, however, the most famous college star joined the NFL. Halfback Red Grange signed with the Chicago Bears. The move launched professional football's rise to greatness.

Running back Harold E. "Red" Grange (1903-1991) gained national attention as a football star at the University of Illinois. By joining the NFL, Grange gave the professional football league instant credibility.

EVOLUTION ON TRIAL

British scientist Charles Darwin first suggested the theory of evolution in the 1850s. His idea sparked a debate that continues even today. In 1925, Darwin's theory was once again in the headlines. It became the focus of one of the most famous court trials in American history.

Darwin said that all species—including humans—evolved (developed) from common ancestors. The concept defied the Bible's description of human creation. Some people also misunderstood the theory of evolution. They thought it meant that humans had descended from monkeys. For these reasons, the state of Tennessee enacted a special law in March 1925. It banned the

English naturalist Charles Darwin (1809–1882) became famous for his theory that all species of life evolved over time from common ancestors.

Darwin developed his ideas about evolution after studying birds, iguanas, and other creatures on the Galápagos Islands during the 1830s.

teaching of evolution in public schools. A twenty-four-year-old teacher named John Scopes felt that the law was wrong. He defied the ban. Four months later, Scopes went on trial for teaching evolution in science class.

The "Scopes Monkey Trial" brought world attention to the sleepy town of Dayton, Tennessee. More than two hundred newspaper reporters covered the event. Radio stations carried it nationwide. In the end, the eight-day trial did little to resolve the evolution controversy. John Scopes was found guilty of violating state law. The judge ordered him to pay a $100 fine. But Scopes's conviction was later overturned because the jury rather than the judge should have set the fine. Tennessee's law prohibiting the teaching of evolution was not repealed until 1967.

Clarence Darrow (1857–1938), one of the most famous lawyers of the 1920s, addresses the judge during the Scopes Monkey Trial. Despite Darrow's arguments, the judge found Scopes guilty.

A photo of the antibiotic *Penicillin notatum*, magnified to six hundred times its actual size. Penicillin was discovered in 1928. However, it took more than a decade before scientists began to understand how penicillin could be used to reduce infection by destroying harmful bacteria within a person's body. (Inset) Dr. Alexander Fleming (1881–1955) holds a petri dish in his laboratory.

Scientific Triumphs

The 1920s saw many important scientific and medical advances. Chief among them were the discovery of penicillin and insulin.

When a person is wounded, there is a risk of infection. Bacteria can enter the body through the break in the skin. If not properly treated, infection can lead to further injury and even death. A Scottish biologist named Alexander Fleming knew of the horrible suffering caused by infected wounds. During

Scientist and inventor George Washington Carver (1864–1943) is pictured in the center, front row, of this photograph. The others shown are members of his research staff at the Tuskegee Institute, a school for African Americans. By the early 1920s, Carver had become famous for his efforts to develop new uses for such crops as peanuts, sweet potatoes, and soybeans.

World War I, he treated many wounded soldiers. After the war, Fleming worked to find a better way of stopping bacterial infection. Years passed with only moderate success.

One day in 1928, Fleming was working in his lab. He noticed that mold had grown on some of his bacteria samples. Fleming was annoyed because he thought his experiments were ruined. Then he noticed something unusual. The bacteria would not grow wherever the mold was present. Fleming realized that the mold could be used to prevent bacterial infection. He identified the mold as belonging to the *Penicillium* family. Accordingly, he called his discovery "penicillin." It was the first in a class of drugs known as the antibiotics. Penicillin would save countless lives.

Diabetes is another dangerous medical problem. People with diabetes are in need of insulin. Without insulin, these people face illness, coma, and death. Before 1922, doctors had no way to give insulin to diabetes patients. In that year, scientists at the University of Toronto in Canada made an amazing

In 1926, John L. Baird (1888–1946) demonstrated the first working television broadcast in London. He is pictured here with a version of his machine, called a "televisor."

A statue of the famous physicist Albert Einstein (1879-1955). In 1921, Einstein received the Nobel Prize in Physics for his theory of relativity, which describes the relationship between matter, time, and space.

breakthrough. They learned how to change animal insulin for human use. Many of the diabetes patients were children. Upon receiving insulin injections, they quickly started to get better. Diabetes no longer meant a slow and certain death. Instead, it became a highly treatable disease. Today, millions of diabetic people lead happy and normal lives thanks to insulin injections.

KING TUT'S TOMB DISCOVERED

Ancient Egyptian kings were called pharaohs. Tutankhamun was a very young pharaoh who lived in the fourteenth century B.C.E. The exact dates are not known, but some sources suggest he ruled from 1343 to 1333 B.C.E. Experts believe he died as a teenager due to complications from an injury. In 1922, British archaeologists uncovered his hidden tomb. The discovery made Tutankhamun the best-known pharaoh. It also sparked the modern world's fascination with ancient Egypt.

Archaeologist Howard Carter found the tomb buried beneath the Egyptian desert. Carter and his financial sponsor, Lord Carnarvon, were the first people to enter the elaborate gravesite in over 3,000 years. Once inside, they found thousands of priceless objects. They also found Tutankhamun's mummy and his now-famous gold mask.

Howard Carter discovered this gold mask of Tutankhamun's mummy when he opened the ancient pharaoh's tomb in 1922.

SECRET CULTURE OF ALCOHOL

Prohibition, the national ban on liquor, went into effect in 1920. It sought to rid American society of the evils of alcohol. Instead, it created a secret culture of defiance and crime.

Before Prohibition, law-abiding companies made and sold alcohol. Once liquor became illegal, those companies switched to other products. Some Americans, however, still desired a drink. Outlaws and gangsters stepped in to meet the demand for alcohol. They smuggled liquor into the country from Canada and overseas. They sold it in secret nightclubs called "speakeasies." (Customers were told to "speak easy,"

A flapper shows off a tire cover with an anti-Prohibition slogan, circa 1929. The Crusaders was an organization formed to support the repeal of the Eighteenth Amendment.

or quietly, when ordering a drink.) Thousands of these clubs operated across the nation. In addition to drinks, many offered live bands and other entertainment. Alcohol, music, and speakeasies helped define 1920s American culture.

Prohibition was a failure. As the decade drew to a close, it became the law that nobody (except for criminals) wanted. Police found it difficult to enforce. Gangsters bribed corrupt public officials. As a result, speakeasy owners knew of police raids in advance. Gradually, Americans began calling on their government to end the ban on alcohol.

Prohibition officers haul barrels of illegal liquor from the basement of a Washington, D.C., lunchroom, April 1923.

One of the most famous speakeasy operators was a former silent film actress, Texas Guinan (1884–1933). She ran several illegal nightclubs in New York during Prohibition. When one club was raided, she would open another at a new address.

Tuning in to Radio

Radio was still a new invention in the 1920s. During World War I, private citizens were not allowed to own radio sets. The government feared that spies would use them to send messages to the enemy. After the war, the ban was lifted. Anyone could own a radio. Soon, shows were filling the airwaves.

America's first radio station went on the air in November 1920. It was station KDKA from Pittsburgh, Pennsylvania. KDKA played music and news from the roof of the Westinghouse Electric Corporation factory. The little station was actually an experiment. Westinghouse hoped it would boost radio sales.

The plan worked. People started tuning in to listen. More stations suddenly popped up all across the country. Within two years, over 60,000 American homes had a radio. By 1929, there were more than 10 million sets in use. Radio quickly became the nation's premier source of news and entertainment, including music, sports, and fictional tales.

Between 1923 and 1930, an estimated 60 percent of American families purchased radios. Interest in the new devices led to the establishment of new radio stations throughout the country.

Music programs were among the most popular radio shows during the 1920s. There was something for everyone: classical, jazz, opera, and country. One long-running radio program was the Grand Ole Opry, which was broadcast from Nashville every Friday and Saturday night beginning in 1925.

Here Come the "Talkies"

Early movies had no sound. Audiences could not hear the actors speaking. That ended in 1927 with a film called The Jazz Singer. It was the first feature-length film with dialogue and singing that could be heard. Moviegoers went wild for the "talkies." Silent films quickly vanished from the silver screen.

The Jazz Singer was the first full-length movie in which the actors could be heard singing and speaking. It starred Al Jolson, the most popular entertainer of the 1920s.

Lucky Lindy Flies the Atlantic

In 1927, pilot Charles Lindbergh became the first person ever to fly across the Atlantic Ocean alone. His nonstop solo flight made him a world celebrity. It also made flying a popular form of travel. Before Lindbergh's feat, few people ever considered climbing aboard an airplane. It simply seemed too dangerous.

Charles Lindbergh (1902–1974) poses with his small airplane, the *Spirit of St. Louis*, in May 1927.

Charles Lindbergh had never been afraid of airplanes. At age twenty, he dropped out of college to attend flying school. Afterward, he worked as a stunt pilot. He also delivered airmail. Then Lindbergh began planning a nonstop flight from New York to Paris. There was a $25,000 prize for the first pilot to succeed. Many had tried before and failed. Some pilots had even died during the attempt. Regardless, Lindbergh was confident. His plane was the single-engine *Spirit of St. Louis*. He took off from New York on the morning of May 20, 1927. He touched down in Paris more than thirty-three hours later. The entire world celebrated.

The *Spirit of St. Louis* was less than twenty-eight feet long, and could attain a maximum speed of about 130 miles per hour. Today, Lindbergh's aircraft is on display at the Smithsonian Institution in Washington, D.C.

Charles Lindbergh returned home to parades and medals. The American public cheered its new hero. Many people instantly lost their fear of flying. Suddenly, everybody wanted to be like "Lucky Lindy."

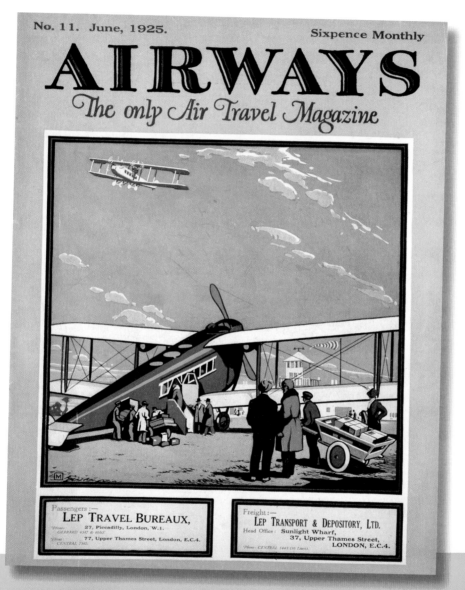

During the 1920s, most airlines focused on carrying mail, rather than passengers. But a few passenger lines were started during the decade. The Ford Motor Company produced a sturdy, reliable airplane called the Trimotor, which could carry up to twelve passengers. This is an example of an air travel magazine from June 1925.

The Japanese Emperor Hirohito (1901–1989), pictured here in coronation robes. On December 25, 1926, Hirohito was crowned as the one hundred and twenty-fourth emperor of Japan.

HIROHITO ASCENDS TO THE THRONE

The 1920s were a difficult period in Japan. There was political turmoil. Many people had no work. An earthquake destroyed the cities of Tokyo and Yokohama in 1923. Three years later, a prince named Hirohito became emperor. The Japanese people hoped that his rule would make life better. Unfortunately, it was about to get much worse.

This Japanese print shows a Japanese army attacking German and Austrian forces near Siberia, 1918. During the First World War, Japan sided with the Allied powers—Great Britain, France, Italy, and, later, the United States—against Germany, Austria-Hungary, and the Ottoman Empire. In the Treaty of Versailles, Japan was rewarded with control over Germany's colony in Asia's Shandong peninsula. This helped to establish Japan as a major world power.

Japan had prospered during World War I. Its factories made wartime supplies and weapons for other countries. When the war ended, the demand for Japanese products faded. The factories were forced to lay off their workers. People felt that their elected leaders were not doing enough to ease their suffering. The Japanese military was also unhappy with the nation's elected officials. Army generals did not like Japan's turn toward a more democratic form of government. The generals became bold and aggressive. They stopped following the orders of the government.

In December 1926, Emperor Yoshihito died. His twenty-five-year-old son, Hirohito, became the new emperor. Hirohito had trained for this role his entire life. He had studied in Japan and Europe. He was the first member of the imperial family to travel beyond Japan's home islands. As emperor, he would be the country's supreme ruler. However, he would not be allowed to make many decisions. Japanese legend held that the emperor descended from the

The rising sun flag was the official banner of Japan's military forces. Success in wars with China (1894–95) and Russia (1904–05), gave the military great influence over Japan's government. Over time, the young emperor adopted the military viewpoint.

Hirohito reviews Japanese troops, circa 1928. As the emperor began appearing in public wearing a military uniform and carrying a sword, many Japanese took this as a sign that Hirohito supported the military position and favored war.

gods. Accordingly, it was felt that he should not be bothered with trivial matters. Japanese military leaders used this belief to slowly take control of the nation. Privately, Hirohito complained of the military's growing power. Yet he did little to stop it.

In the coming years, Japanese society would fall under the spell of the armed forces. Factories would produce nothing but war supplies. Japanese citizens were lulled into believing that foreigners were inferior. The army said that the Japanese Empire needed to expand. People were told to work hard and think of nothing but the glory of Japan. Emperor Hirohito seemed to support these warlike ideas. He often appeared in public wearing a military uniform.

During the 1930s, Japan would invade China. Japan's leaders also sought to expand their control into the Pacific Ocean. In December 1941, Japanese forces would attack the United States at Pearl Harbor, Hawaii. These actions would cause much death and suffering. Under Hirohito's rule, Japan would know the darkest time in its long history.

ARRIVAL OF ART DECO

Architects design buildings. Their work is both a science and an art. A building must be safe and practical. It should also be pleasing to the eye. In the mid-1920s, a unique style of architecture and design emerged. Known as art deco, it combined dazzling beauty with everyday function.

The art deco movement began in France. It first appeared at a Paris arts show in 1925. Previous styles used natural curves and flowery designs. Art deco was different. It favored sleek lines and modern patterns. Art deco imitated the grace and speed of machines. Designers used elegant materials such as glass, stainless steel, and inlaid wood. The look was both fresh and luxurious.

New York City became the heart of the art deco movement. New skyscrapers were built in the art deco style. These included the Chrysler Building, which was begun in 1928. When it was finished two years later, the building was the tallest manmade structure in the world. But the Chrysler Building would soon be dwarfed by another skyscraper in the art deco style: the Empire State Building.

The Chrysler Building is a famous example of a skyscraper built in the Art Deco style. The building is 1,047 feet tall. It is still considered to be one of the finest buildings in the city.

Union Station in Omaha, Nebraska, is considered one of the best examples of Art Deco architecture in the Midwest. Construction on the building began in 1929.

Art deco quickly spread across the country. It could be seen in the design of train stations and movie theaters. It also influenced furniture and jewelry, and even automobiles. Art deco remained a driving force in design until the end of the 1930s.

Buildings constructed in the Art Deco style typically utilize geometric shapes in a symmetrical, stylized way. Today, Ocean Drive in Miami has a high concentration of Art Deco buildings. The Miami Beach Art Deco District was placed on the National Register of Historic Places in 1979.

Arrival of Art Deco

RISE OF THE GANGSTERS

Al Capone (1899–1947) was the most infamous gangster of the 1920s.

Gangs of violent criminals were very powerful during the 1920s. They grew rich by providing illegal liquor and by controlling other illegal activities, such as gambling. Mobsters used bribery and fear to suppress the local police. In some cities—such as Detroit, New York, and Chicago—powerful gangs controlled entire neighborhoods.

America's best-known gangster was Al Capone. He ruled Chicago for most of the decade. Capone began his criminal career in New York. At age twenty, he moved to Chicago. There he quickly amassed wealth and power. He owned a network of speakeasies and casinos. Capone dealt ruthlessly with his rivals. However, in public he tried to appear generous and kindhearted. Many city residents were fooled by this ruse. They admired and respected him.

The bullet-riddled bodies of slain gangsters lie on the floor of a Chicago warehouse, February 14, 1929. The St. Valentine's Day Massacre was the most notorious gang killing of the decade. The dead men were members of a gang run by Capone's rival, Bugs Moran.

Five New York mobsters—Dominick Odierno, Michael Basile, Pasquale Del Greco, Frank Giordano, and Vincent "Mad Dog" Coll—are lined up after being arrested.

A turning point came in February 1929. Al Capone's men executed seven members of a rival gang in cold blood. It became known as the St. Valentine's Day Massacre. After this slaughter, the federal government began investigating Capone. He was charged with income tax evasion. Capone was sentenced to eleven years in prison.

Despite Al Capone's imprisonment, gangsters continued to flourish. Prohibition had the unexpected effect of helping organized crime take root in America. It would thrive for the rest of the Prohibition era and well beyond.

Bewildered investors crowd the streets outside the New York Stock Exchange building on Tuesday, October 29, 1929.

THE GREAT DEPRESSION BEGINS

The Roaring Twenties were a time of revelry. Nobody knew that the party would end suddenly. The U.S. stock market crashed in the fall of 1929. It was the start of a worldwide financial collapse.

When people spend more money than they earn, they are said to be in debt. Falling too deeply into debt can leave people unable to repay the money they owe. During the 1920s, many people were deep in debt. They wanted to buy the latest cars, appliances, and gadgets. However, they did not earn enough money from work to pay for these things. They therefore chose to borrow money.

Republican Herbert Hoover (1874–1964) was elected president in November 1928. As president, Hoover was criticized for not doing enough to help Americans fallen on hard times after the stock market crash.

A newspaper headline from "Black Thursday," October 24, 1929.

Nations can fall into debt too. After World War I, the nations of Europe needed money to repair the damage caused by the war. They borrowed heavily from American banks. Some of these countries, especially Germany, were unable to repay their loans. This placed strain on the U.S. banking system.

Despite these troubles, the U.S. stock market continued to grow. The future seemed bright. People continued to borrow money.

By 1929, there was no more money left to borrow. It seemed as if nearly everyone was in debt. Many people could not afford to pay for past purchases, much less buy new items. Products sat unsold on store shelves, so companies started making less of their products. This meant that fewer workers were needed. As workers were laid off, demand for products dropped even further because people who had lost their jobs had no money to spend. As a result, companies stopped earning profits.

Unemployed men are lined up outside a soup kitchen in Chicago, February 1931. During the Great Depression, between 10 and 25 percent of American workers could not find jobs.

A relief agency distributes supplies to farmers in Arizona. It was not just urban dwellers that suffered during the depression. Farmers were affected, as crop prices dropped by more than 50 percent.

This, in turn, caused people to lose confidence in the value of stocks—shares in a company that may be bought or sold. Worried investors began selling their shares, causing the stock market to plunge on October 24, 1929. People grimly nicknamed it Black Thursday. The following Monday, the stock market fell even further. Then, on October 29—Black Tuesday—panic set in. Everyone was trying to sell, and the stock market crashed. It lost $14 billion in value in one day. Family fortunes and life savings instantly disappeared.

America's stock market crash was not the cause of the Great Depression. Instead, it was the first symptom. After the stock market crash, people quickly rushed to withdraw their money from banks, which did not have enough cash on hand to pay everybody. Many banks closed. Businesses could not get the money they needed to keep operating, either. As businesses failed, more than 15 million people lost their jobs. Like a disease, the depression spread around the globe. The glee of the Roaring Twenties was over. All that remained was hopelessness and despair. Recovery would take more than a decade.

LOOKING AHEAD

The decade 1920–1929 is often viewed as a wild and happy time in the United States. Americans were relieved that the Great War was over. By 1920, they were ready to celebrate and enjoy life. The "Roaring Twenties" were a glamorous and exciting time. People avidly followed the accomplishments of their favorite athletes. Charles Lindbergh was celebrated as a national hero for his solo flight across the Atlantic. Americans enjoyed attending movies and listening to radio broadcasts. Women gained new rights and a greater role in public society.

Beneath the glittering exterior, however, there were many problems. Many people went deeply into debt purchasing consumer products, like washing machines and record players. Prohibition led to an increase in the power and influence of criminal gangs. At the end of the decade, the U.S. stock market crashed. This was the first crisis of the Great Depression.

The next decade, 1930–1939, would be a troubled time for the United States and the world. Millions of people were out of work, and could barely find enough food to survive. In 1932, Franklin D. Roosevelt was elected president of the United States. Roosevelt soon created a bold plan called the New Deal, which he hoped would end the Great Depression. Roosevelt spoke often to the nation on the radio. He encouraged people and gave many Americans hope that better times were ahead.

Despite the president's efforts, the Depression would continue through the decade. In other countries, the financial crisis created political turmoil. In Germany and Japan, dangerous men used the chaos to seize power. As the 1930s ended, the world plunged into a second World War. World War II would become the deadliest conflict in human history.

African-American migrants are photographed outside the shacks where they live in Florida. The hard times of the 1930s forced many people to take temporary work on farms, traveling from place to place as the seasons changed.

Chronology

1920—Prohibition goes into effect in January. The Nineteenth Amendment is ratified, enabling women to vote. The League of Women Voters is founded. Babe Ruth is sold by the Boston Red Sox to the New York Yankees.

1921—Warren Harding takes office as America's twenty-ninth president. In May, Congress creates a system for controlling immigration.

1922—Doctors begin treating diabetes patients with insulin injections. The Senate starts investigating the Teapot Dome oil leases. Tutankhamun's tomb is discovered in Egypt. In October, Benito Mussolini becomes Italy's prime minister.

1923—President Harding dies in August. Calvin Coolidge succeeds him. A devastating earthquake shatters the Japanese cities of Tokyo and Yokohama. Adolf Hitler attempts his Beer Hall Putsch in November.

1924—Hitler serves a nine-month prison term for treason. In Wyoming, Nellie Tayloe Ross is elected, becoming the nation's first female governor. Calvin Coolidge is elected president of the United States.

1925—In July, the Scopes trial takes place in Dayton, Tennessee. Halfback Red Grange signs with the Chicago Bears.

1926—Gene Tunney defeats Jack Dempsey for the world heavyweight boxing title. Hirohito ascends to the Japanese throne in December.

1927—In May, Charles Lindbergh makes first nonstop solo flight across the Atlantic Ocean, flying from New York to Paris. *The Jazz Singer* marks the end of the silent film era.

1928—Republican Herbert Hoover is elected president. Scottish biologist Alexander Fleming discovers penicillin.

1929—Al Capone's hit men carry out the St. Valentine's Day Massacre in Chicago. Albert B. Fall is convicted of accepting bribes in the Teapot Dome scandal. The U.S. stock market crashes in October.

GLOSSARY

architect—A person who designs buildings and other large structures.

bacteria—Very tiny organisms that can be found nearly everywhere on earth.

bribe—Money or other benefit given to influence a person making a decision.

communism—A form of government in which all goods and property are supposed to be shared equally.

immigrant—A person who moves from one country to another.

infection—An invasion of the body by bacteria or other tiny organisms.

lease—An agreement to borrow or rent.

liquor—An alcoholic beverage.

ratify—To approve or confirm.

speakeasy—A place where liquor was sold during Prohibition. These bars were illegal, so it was necessary to speak quietly or to "speak easy."

stock market—A place where people buy and sell shares of ownership in companies.

suffrage—The right to vote.

treason—A betrayal of one's country.

FURTHER READING

Bobek, Milan, editor. *Decades of the Twentieth Century: The 1920s*. Pittsburgh, Pa.: Eldorado Ink, 2005.

Gourley, Catherine. *Flappers and the New American Woman*. Breckenridge, Colo.: Twenty-First Century Books, 2007.

Fitzgerald, Stephanie. *The Scopes Trial: The Battle over Teaching Evolution*. Mankato, Minn.: Compass Point Books, 2007.

Hixson, Walter L. *Charles A. Lindbergh: Lone Eagle*. 3rd ed. New York: Longman, 2006.

Landau, Elaine. *Warren G. Harding*. Minneapolis, Minn.: Lerner Publications, 2004.

Meachen Rau, Dana. *Great Women of the Suffrage Movement*. Mankato, Minn.: Compass Point Books, 2006.

Slavicek, Louise Chipley. *The Prohibition Era: Temperance in the United States*. New York: Chelsea House, 2008.

Streissguth, Thomas. *The Roaring Twenties*. 2nd ed. New York: Facts on File, 2006.

INTERNET RESOURCES

<http://www.charleslindbergh.com/>
Visit this fact-filled site to read about the adventures of pilot Charles Lindbergh. It includes newspaper reports of his historic flight.

<http://prohibition.osu.edu/>
The Ohio State University presents this complete history of Prohibition in America.

<http://www.nytimes.com/library/financial/index-1929-crash.html>
This *New York Times* site displays the newspaper's front page on October 30, 1929. It was the day after Black Tuesday, when the U.S. stock market crashed.

INDEX

PICTURE CREDITS